Political Cartoons of 1998

Compiled by Jane Newton, Centre for the Study of Cartoons and Caricature,

University of Kent at Canterbury

Centre for the Study of Cartoons and Caricature

University of Kent at Canterbury

The Centre holds an archive of over 85,000 original cartoons and caricatures which date back to 1903 and have been published in the major British newspapers and periodicals.

The cartoons are available to exhibition venues around the world. The Centre also runs a picture library service and undertakes commissioned research.

The largest and most heavily used part of the collection concerns political and social subjects, although there are also a substantial number of strip and gag cartoons. Cartoonists represented in the collection number around sixty and include Sidney 'George' Strube, David Low, Vicky [Victor Weisz] and Ralph Steadman.

The catalogue records include the name of the artist, the date, the publication, the personalities depicted and the subject matter. This information, along with the image of the cartoon, is available on a computerised database which can be searched quickly and easily.

The archive is supported by a reference library of about 4,000 books on cartoons, caricature, cartoonists and humour.

The Centre relies entirely on grants and donations for its funding. The support of cartoonists in depositing their work with us is fundamental to our work. Collecting and cataloguing British cartoons for the enjoyment and enlightenment of future generations, and encouraging the study and research of the collection, is our purpose.

Anyone interested in sponsoring, supporting, donating to, talking about, studying at, visiting, collaborating with the Centre should contact Jane Newton, Curator, Centre for the Study of Cartoons and Caricature, 01227 823127 phone and fax. Email J.M.Newton@ukc.ac.uk
Website http://libservb.ukc.ac.uk/cartoons/

UNIVERSITY OF KENT
AT CANTERBURY ■■■■

Preface

'Honk if you'll miss her!' Steve Bell's juggernaut truck, blazoning this message, roars up the motorway to Northants in a cartoon about Princess Diana's funeral. Whatever future generations make of that emotional time, we can be sure they will turn to cartoons for help. Most cartoon annuals stick to a specific artist – the long series of Giles and Jak, now collectors' items, or the latest Alex. This collection goes much wider. Twenty-four artists from fifteen newspapers give us a variety of viewpoints on people and events, as New Labour settled into office and Bill Clinton protested, in Riddell's pun linking Lewinsky to his student drug days, that he 'didn't impale'.

Cartoons are editorials in pictures. The cartoonist's task is to suggest to us how things are, day by day, and perhaps to add a personal opinion. Over the last twenty-five years the cartoon archive at the University of Kent has been a depository for collections of original drawings, mostly published in the national press during the twentieth century. The computer catalogue, user friendly, cross-referenced in detail and available on the internet, now includes contemporary published cartoons, scanned in on a daily basis. Archive users – teachers, journalists, TV producers, publishers, academics and even GCSE examiners – can therefore quickly identify when, by whom and (above all) why Tony Blair is drawn as a cricket ball, John Prescott as a hedgehog and Hague as a Teletubby doll. (For answers, see within.) Publication of this anthology is a convenient by-product.

Anthologies give cartoons an afterlife. Even after a year, these ones do not seem quite the same as they did. The Diana cartoons, for example, increasingly help us not to relive the episode but to re-evaluate our reactions. After the accident cartoonists, often critical of her while she was alive, blamed photographers, the tabloid press, an obsessive public and/or the royal family. In a typical example of inventive imagery, Scarfe turns the massed bunches of flowers into a tidal wave, looming over the fleeing Windsors. History will make its own judgements about blame. Scarfe's image will be an evocative and readily understood piece of evidence.

The New Labour government gave cartoonists a fresh cast of leading characters. As they grew familiar, the cartoon versions became simplified. Blair is now all ears and teeth. Ears add absurdity and assist ridicule, but teeth are more complex. Teeth feature both in smiles and sneers, and a smile itself can be either warm or menacing. Bell's Blair wears a smile which, topped by a spherical eye, gives him the 'psychotic glint' which Bell used also to give Mrs Thatcher. Rowson's Blair increasingly appears in almost two-dimensional profile, it seems, with a smile some way towards mania and built like a cascade of piano keys. Brookes' Blair has no teeth, the smile is a gap, a blank space. William Hague, in contrast, presents a gift to caricaturists in his remarkable forehead.

While caricature may help, cartoons principally work through imagery. The anthology therefore shows people in an astonishing variety of roles chosen by the artists to make a point about their behaviour. Blair appears as a doctor, juggler, nanny, charioteer, cowboy, baby, train driver, prophet, photographer, pop star, stripper and puppet (Rupert Murdoch pulling the strings). He walks on water (till Bernie Ecclestone sinks him). He is clad in armour and rides a white charger. He is a cricket ball spun by Alastair Campbell.

Historical and cultural comparisons are another common source of imagery. Blair is Scrooge. Hague is a Teletubby. Riddell draws a fine Welsh dragon, as Blair squeezes a close referendum victory. Michael Portillo strips off his 'old morality', as in the popular film, *The Full Monty*. Helmut Kohl tumbles into the sea, in a pastiche of Tenniel's famous *Punch* cartoon about the resignation of Bismarck, 'Dropping the Pilot'. In something of a tour de force, Brookes fits at least half-a-dozen members of the government and opposition into 'Dan Blair', a parody of the celebrated 'Dan Dare' strip in the comic *Eagle*. This is demanding a lot from *Times* readers, since *Eagle* ceased publication in 1969. Such puns are a cartoonist's standby. Brookes gives us the Socialism Exclusion Unit, for example. But they risk making a cartoon little more than an illustrated joke, like the Clinton 'impale' pun. Brookes has also made a speciality of 'Nature Notes', using the traditional device of turning humans into other creatures. So we see John Major as a cricket, Jonathan Aitken as a louse and John Prescott as a grumblebee.

These techniques have long been the cartoonist's stock in trade. The trick is to find new ideas and fresh images. One measure of the success of the cartoons in this collection is that the freshness endures. The publication of the volume is above all, therefore, a tribute to the cartoonists' art.

Colin Seymour-Ure

New Labour faced accusations of creating a 'Nanny State', with a 'holier than thou' doctrine embodied in their Election Manifesto. Cummings depicted Margaret Thatcher as the Nanny of her Cabinet after the Conservative's election victory in 1979.

The recently elected Conservative Leader, William Hague and his Party Chairman Cecil Parkinson,
with nothing new to sell after the 1997 General Election disaster, fantasised about the road to recovery
after winning the Uxbridge by-election.

The Northern Ireland Secretary, Mo Mowlam, held her first face-to-face meeting with a
delegation from Sinn Fein that included their leader Gerry Adams, Martin McGuinness and a
convicted IRA gun runner.

Following a Sunday newspaper article on his involvement with his Commons secretary, Gaynor Regan, the Foreign Secretary, Robin Cook, announced that his marriage of twenty-eight years was over. Tony Blair defended Cook and made it clear that it was a personal matter, and that there was no question of his being forced to resign. The Conservatives accused Labour of using double standards.

Diana, Princess of Wales, was ardently pursued by the paparazzi, keen to report the progress of her romantic link with Dodi Fayed, millionaire playboy and son of the Harrods owner Mohammed al-Fayed. This prescient cartoon records Diana's and Dodi's visit to her clairvoyant, Rita Rogers.

MUSICAL CHAIRS

Although no campaigning among Labour party members is allowed when standing for the National Executive Committee, Peter Mandelson courted publicity whilst 'in charge' during Tony Blair's summer holiday. However, the modernising face of New Labour was subsequently rejected by the party's grassroots who voted by 15,000 in favour of the former GLC leader, 'Red' Ken Livingstone, to fill the seat vacated by Gordon Brown on the NEC.

The rivalry between John Prescott, Deputy Prime Minister, and Peter Mandelson intensified
with Prescott naming an aggressive Chinese mitten crab Peter. Prescott's proposed transport policy
included a new orbital rail route around London to relieve congestion and to encourage freight
traffic off the roads.

Labour's ethical foreign policy pledges began to look hollow as the government sponsored an international arms fair and granted export licences for more Hawk jets to Indonesia. Over 200,000 people have been killed in East Timor and internal dissent has been suppressed in parts of Indonesia.

On August 31st, Diana, Princess of Wales, Dodi Fayed and his chauffeur Henri Paul died in a late
night car crash following a high speed chase through Paris, while being pursued by paparazzi. Diana's
bodyguard, Trevor Rees Jones was the only survivor.

Shortly before her death, Diana, Princess of Wales, gave an interview to the French newspaper
Le Monde and lashed out at the British press. In the days immediately after her death public
reaction focused angrily on the tabloid press and celebrity magazines, and their fervent demand
for paparazzi photos.

Diana Princess of Wales' funeral took place in Westminster Abbey. After the service the coffin was driven up the M1 to Northants for a private burial at Althorp, the Spencer home. The referendum on Scottish devolution went ahead on September 11th, leaving just four days for campaigners to get their message across.

An introduction to Brookes' regular *Saturday Times* cartoon strip 'Dan Blair – Pilot for the Foreseeable Future'. The series is a pastiche of the *Eagle* comic strip 'Dan Dare'. The *Eagle* ceased publication in 1969.

Thousands of floral tributes, letters, cards and toys were piled up outside Buckingham Palace and
Kensington Palace, as expressions of personal grief.

The Royal Family came under strong criticism for their initial adherence to protocol and avoidance of showing their sorrow publicly. Protocol was seen to deny 'the people's' wishes that the flag be flown at half-mast over Buckingham Palace, as a mark of respect, despite the Queen not being in residence.

Bonnie Prince Donald

Diana's death overshadowed the Scottish devolution referendum campaign, but the Yes – Yes camp won the day with 4-1 voting in favour of the Scottish Parliament but only 2-1 voting in favour of tax-varying powers. Many Nationalists felt that the powers of the new Scottish Assembly did not go far enough in the crusade for Scottish independence.

New Labour, New Britain; Blair's prime ministerial style was seen to develop in the post-Diana age.
Blair attempted to embody the new values of caring, sharing …. and crying.

Blair seized the opportunity presented by the mood of the nation and guided the Royals towards a 'New' Monarchy, less obsessed with protocol.

The Welsh devolution referendum caused little excitement, with barely half the Welsh voters turning out to vote for a national Welsh assembly. The 'Yes' vote barely won by 0.6%.

Labour's first party conference as the party of government, for eighteen years. The mood was jubilant
and there was little dissent from the floor.

In an extraordinary pledge to deliver full employment in the twenty-first century, Gordon Brown set himself the unenviable task of finding nearly one million jobs over the next few years.

The Conservative party, now severely depleted after their election disaster, gathered for their annual party conference in Blackpool, the first in opposition since 1978.

William Hague attempted to 'young down' his party, beginning with the now legendary baseball cap
and a visit to Thorpe Park during the summer.

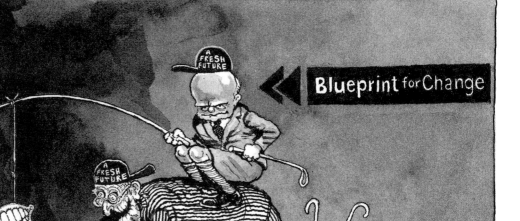

William Hague was forced to disown senior Conservative 'dinosaurs' for clumsy meddling on the
party conference fringe. The controversial views of Lord Tebbit and Alan Clark overshadowed the
Tory Leader's efforts to put his party on the road back to power with the conference slogan,
'A Fresh Future'.

THE FULL MONTY

Michael Portillo did 'the full monty', and stripped away the archaic Conservative notions of sexual morality. At a crowded fringe meeting at the Conservative conference, he championed single parent families, unwed couples and by implication, gays.

'Well, someone must have a better solution than "smack 'em around a bit"'

Michael Portillo's renunciation of Victorian family values and his embrace of single parent families was seen by many to herald a new dawn in Conservative thought on sexual and social morality.

"I'M ONLY BEING INCLUSIVE..."

Tony Blair was heckled by a crowd of loyalists in East Belfast, as he became the first British Prime Minister to meet Irish Republican leaders since the partition of Ireland. He shook hands with Gerry Adams, leader of Sinn Fein, with whom he spent some ten minutes whilst on a visit to the Stormont talks in Belfast.

The Queen's state visit to India was beset with protocol disputes and diplomatic rows. The exclusion from a state banquet, at the eleventh hour, of every British diplomat except the High Commissioner and the cancelling of a speech the Queen was due to make in Madras were a further source of embarrassment for Robin Cook. Cook was already accused, both here and in India, of mishandling British politics on Kashmir.

The hazards of 'spinning'. The Chancellor, Gordon Brown, stressed the need for a period of stability after ten million pounds was wiped off share prices at the London Stock Exchange. Dubbed "Brown Monday", the collapse was triggered by conflicting statements to the press from Brown's press secretary, Charlie Whelan, on Britain's policy about European Monetary Union.

Tony Blair placed his personal authority behind Gordon Brown's attempt to defuse speculation over
Britain's Euro currency policy. Blair promised a "defensive and detailed" statement from Gordon
Brown in the Commons.

"DIDN'T WANT TO BE A MEMBER ANYWAY."

Kenneth Clarke, the former Conservative Chancellor, confirmed his disagreement with the party's
Euro-sceptic stance and called on Tony Blair to mobilise a cross party campaign to secure a 'yes' vote
in a referendum on joining the single European currency before the next election. Despite resignations
and a revolt led by Michael Heseltine, William Hague stated that he was determined to stand firm on
opposition to the single European currency. He warned those who disagreed with his stance to resign
rather that generate continuing tension.

Michael Foster's Private Members Bill, the Wild Mammals (Hunting with Dogs) Bill was published, as a poll showed that a significant majority supported the ban – even among country dwellers. On the 29th of November 260 MPs voted in favour of the ban in a packed Commons chamber. In the USA nanny Louise Woodward was convicted of second-degree murder for the death of Matthew Eappon, who died from a head injury thought to have been caused by being thrown to the ground.

THE CHEQUERED FLAG

The government's policy of exempting Formula One motor racing from the ban on tobacco
advertising in sport came under attack when it was revealed that Formula One boss Bernie Ecclestone
had made a donation of one million pounds to the Labour party before the general election.

The deification of Tony Blair since his election victory was tarnished as he made a public admission that he was wrong not to own up to the one million pound donation by Bernie Ecclestone as soon as the government changed its policy on tobacco advertising for Formula One racing.

True blue Conservative Winchester turned its back on the new Conservatives in a by-election
and returned a Liberal Democrat with a majority of 21,000, wiping out the Conservatives' 1992
majority of 10,000. Demand for Teletubby dolls, however, was high in the run-up to Christmas.

FINANCE CHIEF VERY SORRY, BUT FOR NOW THERE'S NOT MUCH MORE HE CAN DO...

The president of Yamaichi Securities wept and begged for work for his seven and a half thousand employees, as his firm collapsed with liabilities of twenty-four billion dollars. The Chancellor, in his pre-budget report, announced a cash injection into the welfare state. However, he warned, the strategy could easily be blown off course by unjustified wage demands, and he stressed that the alternative to pay restraint from the boardroom to the shop floor would be higher interest rates.

The crisis gripping the world financial system deepened as talks between the South Korean
government and the International Monetary Fund stalled over conditions for a twelve billion pound
rescue package. In London fifteen billion pounds was said to have been wiped off shares as the stock
market reeled at the collapse of the Asian economies.

Following Peter Mandelson's reference to the scheme in a Fabian Lecture in August, Tony Blair launched the 'Social Exclusion Unit', declaring that it would have the remit of co-ordinating the Labour Party's 'assault' on poverty. 'Old' Labour MPs Ken Livingstone, Dennis Skinner and Tony Benn looked on as the ethics of socialism were re-vamped.

Forty-seven Labour MPs voted against the Government's proposal to cut single parent benefits, and many more abstained. Neither the Prime Minister nor any of his Cabinet was present to support the Secretary of State for Social Security, Harriet Harman, as she faced the backbench revolt in the Commons.

The meeting between Gerry Adams, Martin McGuinness and Tony Blair in Downing Street was the first between a British Prime Minister and Irish Nationalist leaders in seventy-six years. Blair described the meeting as 'a risk worth taking'.

"If Tiny Tim be like to die, he had better do it, and decrease the surplus population." Scrooge hung his head to hear his own words quoted by the Spirit.
— *A Christmas Carol (2)*

Tony Blair faced the disapproval of the Parliamentary Labour Party as he took personal charge of the benefits reform programme.

Tony Blair stated in *The Sun* that he was being forced to cut benefits because of Labour's promise
"not to let public spending get out of control. … If money was no problem, we would not have
had to do it".

The government's plans to cut disability benefits were met with protestors in wheelchairs being arrested at the gates of Downing Street. A leaked letter by Secretary of State for Education, David Blunkett, exposed the biggest Cabinet split since Labour came to power.

Mo Mowlam, Secretary of State for Northern Ireland, cut short her New Year holiday to hold
crisis talks with security advisers, after the murder of a Catholic man on New Years' eve by
loyalist paramilitaries.

Ater a taped encounter with journalists from *The Mirror*, William Straw, son of Home Secretary, Jack Straw, faced allegations of dealing marijuana. Jack Straw ruled out any form of legalisation of 'soft' drugs. A 'drugs tsar' was appointed the previous October to co-ordinate the fight against drugs.

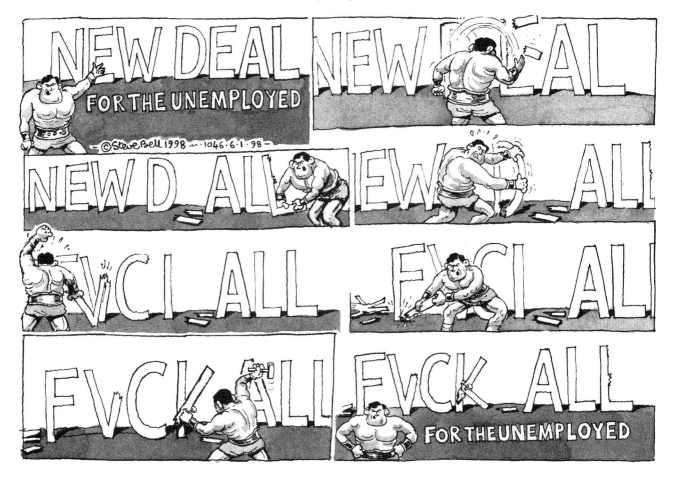

Gordon Brown launched Labour's New Deal for the jobless young with an appeal to employers to join the government's national crusade. The Chancellor confirmed a two hundred million pound extension of the nation-wide pilot scheme as part of the Welfare to Work programme.

Tony Blair set off on a whistle-stop 'welfare roadshow' in an attempt to persuade 'the people' that the fifty-year-old welfare system needed dramatic restructuring. He spoke to Labour activists of a welfare system that has split the nation, "One nation trapped on benefits, the other paying for them".

The publication of Gordon Brown's biography, written by political journalist Paul Routledge, allegedly with the Chancellor's co-operation, intensified what was already perceived as a strained relationship between him and the Prime Minister.

Bill Clinton, renowned for his defence of cannabis smoking "I didn't inhale", constructed
a comparable defence of extra-marital affairs. According to some newspaper reports Clinton assured
Ms Monica Lewinsky that according to the Bible oral sex does not constitute adultery and was,
therefore, permissible.

'Okay Hillary, honey. You take charge. But what can you do that I couldn't?'

Bill Clinton stood accused of carrying on an eighteen month affair inside the White House with
Monica Lewinsky, a twenty-three year old member of staff, and of persuading her to lie under oath,
leave her job and deny that the liaison ever happened. Hillary Clinton stood by her man and appeared
on television, by his side, stating that the scandal was a "right-wing conspiracy".

Tony Blair made an impassioned defence of his plans for radical welfare reform on the second of his 'welfare roadshows'. Blair addressed 400 party members in a hall in Luton and spoke of welfare reform as a means of cutting the tax costs of the average family whilst helping to lift the most vulnerable people in society out of poverty and into work.

Bill Clinton and Tony Blair jointly outlined a plan to deal with Iraq if Saddam Hussein continued to refuse to allow UN weapons inspectors to search the presidential palaces for evidence of chemical weapons and Iraq's manufacturing capability. After talks in Washington an agreement was reached on the types of targets selected for an Anglo-American attack.

Sinn Fein leaders were expelled from the all-party peace talks in Northern Ireland after the RUC confirmed that the IRA had been responsible for the recent murder of a loyalist figure, who was also a suspected drugs dealer.

William Hague re-branded the Conservative party, declaring it to have a "Fresh Future".
He also claimed to have modernised the party by initiating the "most radical reforms since the time
of Disraeli". He set a target of achieving one million party members and was asking them to endorse
his proposal for the 'one man one vote' system to be introduced for party leadership elections.

Tony Blair announced the exhibits and attractions chosen to fill the Millennium Dome.
These would include the "Dreamscape Zone – Dream, imagine and return refreshed", the
"Body Zone -Voyage into the human machine and learn how to get the best from it",
and the "Transaction Zone – See how money and finance are changing your life".

'It's part of the "dreamscape" feature at the Dome, Lord Irvine. People travel in little boats from Greenwich and through your new apartments imagining what it must be like to be disgustingly over-indulged.'

Lord Irvine of Lairg, the Lord Chancellor, was criticised for the extravagant refurbishment of his official residence, reported as costing £650,000 of taxpayers' money. Lord Irvine's new décor was said to include hand-made, reproduction Pugin, flock wallpaper costing £300 a roll. He also planned to borrow works of art from the national galleries.

Frank Field, the Social Security Minister with responsibility for welfare reform, spoke of reports
claiming that he had a low opinion of his senior colleague, Harriet Harman, as "untrue and hurtful".
Around 200,000 people descended on Hyde Park in defence of rural life.
The Countryside March was called in protest at issues such as the proposed banning of hunting
with dogs and plans to give ramblers a statutory 'right to roam'.

Russia joined the US and Britain in backing an arms embargo on Yugoslavia in an attempt to punish Slobodan Milosevic for his brutal crackdown on ethnic Albanians living in the Serbian province of Kosovo.

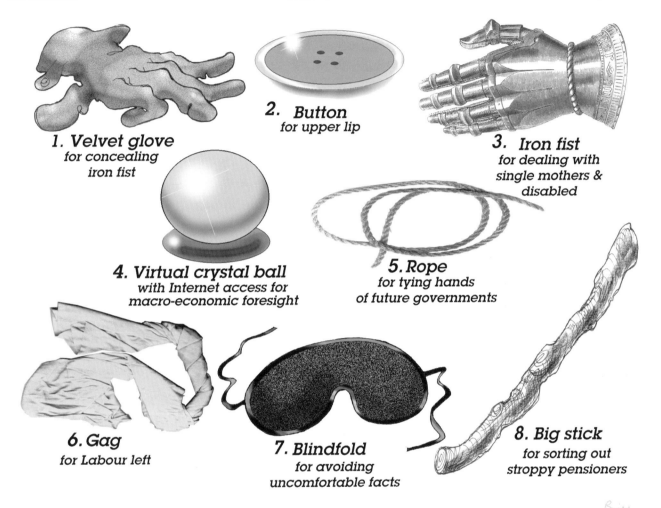

1. Velvet glove
for concealing
iron fist

2. Button
for upper lip

3. Iron fist
for dealing with
single mothers &
disabled

4. Virtual crystal ball
with Internet access for
macro-economic foresight

5. Rope
for tying hands
of future governments

6. Gag
for Labour left

7. Blindfold
for avoiding
uncomfortable facts

8. Big stick
for sorting out
stroppy pensioners

Contents of Budget box.

Gordon Brown's second budget was expected to attack 'the culture of welfare dependency'
and to focus on tax incentives to get people back to work, thus living up to his reputation as
'The Iron Chancellor'.

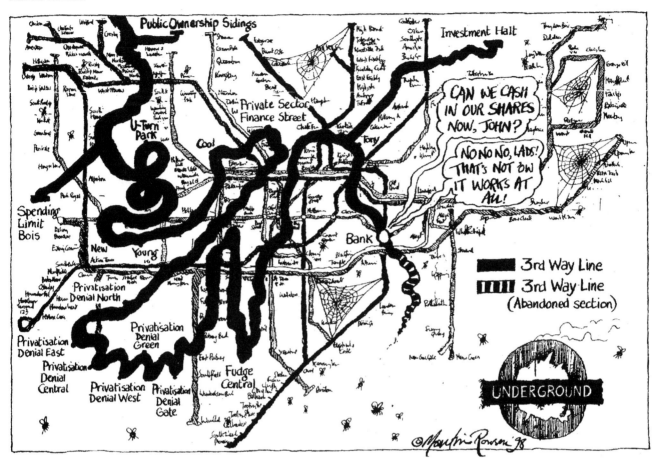

The government announced plans for a partial privatisation of London Underground in an attempt to generate an estimated seven billion pounds needed to improve the service for the network's two and a half million daily passengers.

Frank Field's consultative green paper, "A new contract for welfare", presented an assault against
the work-shy and benefit fraudsters, and took the first steps toward compulsory second pensions.
It claimed to be the first "truly comprehensive review of the welfare state in all its elements
since Beveridge".

Tony Blair's Press Secretary, Alastair Campbell, angrily rejected allegations by William Hague and the
media that he was a liar. He was accused of supervising a campaign of evasion and misinformation
about Blair's telephone conversation with the Italian prime minister, Romano Prodi, which allegedly
touched on Rupert Murdoch's commercial plans in Italy.

Tony Blair promoted 'Cool Britannia' as Robin Cook was appointed to head Panel 2000, a committee made up of businessmen, designers and television stars with the mission to define and market Britain's modern image.

THE PEACE STRAIN

Tony Blair and the Irish Prime Minister, Bertie Ahern, flew to Belfast to hold a series of last minute meetings after the Ulster Unionists flatly rejected the blueprint put forward by the peace talks chairman, Senator George Mitchell.

Feeling the hand of history on his shoulder, Tony Blair wrested an agreement from the Northern
Ireland all-party peace talks.

The Reverend Ian Paisley, leader of the Democratic Unionist Party, declared his intention to campaign for a 'No' vote in the forthcoming referendum on the Good Friday Agreement. Paisley attempted to appeal to the emotions of disaffected unionists. The Environment Agency confirmed that the floods that devastated areas of Britain were the worst in living memory.

Tony Blair flew to Israel and attempted to shake the hand of history once again by securing an
agreement from the Arab and Israeli leaders to hold a summit in London in May. Analysts questioned
the value of the meeting between the Palestinian leader, Yassir Arafat, and the Israeli Prime Minister,
Binyamin Netanyahu, in the absence of any indication that Israel was ready to compromise.

HOMEWORK

New government guidelines stated that four-year-olds should spend twenty minutes a day on homework and sixteen-year-olds two-and-a-half hours. The Health Secretary, Frank Dobson, was jeered by nurses as he apologised for staging their wage rise and admitted that the government's public sector pay policy was no better than that of the previous government.

BUDDIES

The Anglo-American 'special relationship' was strengthened as the Prime Minister defended the government's decision to remain silent over a deal with President Clinton to send weapons-grade nuclear fuel from the former soviet republic of Georgia to the Dounreay reprocessing plant in Scotland.

Tony Blair announced that there were to be no formal celebrations of Labour's first year in office.

Mary Bell, convicted of murder when a child, provoked a moral storm by collaborating with author
Gitta Sereny on a book entitled *Cries Unheard* about her life since she came out of prison for which
she received payment. Jack Straw announced that he was considering extending the Proceeds of Crime
Act, initially drafted to target drug dealers, to include cases such as Mary Bell's. Part of the Good
Friday Agreement reached in April included the early release of IRA prisoners, including those
responsible for bombing the Conservative Party conference in 1984.

A year after the Conservative party's humiliating defeat in the general election things looked no better,
as an opinion poll showed that the Labour party was more popular now than on election day.

Europe's new currency, the euro, faced a crisis, after negotiations over the presidency of the European
Central Bank were overshadowed by a bitter Franco-German row.

'Here it is in a letter I wrote to you two months ago - "My darling Robin. You were wonderful tonight, I love you snookum wookums . . . P.S. Somebody rang about sending arms to Sierra Leone and I said okay . . ."'

After blaming officials for failing to tell ministers that Sandline International, a firm of military 'consultants', had helped to overthrow the Sierra Leone regime earlier this year, Robin Cook tried to extricate the government by telling MP's that there was no evidence that Foreign Office officials had encouraged Sandline International to supply arms to Sierra Leone. Earlier this year, whilst filming a BBC documentary, he said, "I have recognised that you can be a successful Foreign Secretary if you focus on the big questions, not necessarily if you finish the paperwork". Tony Blair sought to turn the government's embarrassment around and Cook dismissed the controversy over the breach of UN sanctions as 'overblown', saying that Foreign Office staff were right to help the counter-coup by President Kabbah.

India exploded five nuclear devices in tests, to a chorus of condemnation led by the United States which is the only country to have used the bomb and has performed over one thousand nuclear test explosions. All economic assistance by the US was stopped and sanctions were imposed.

'Bejasus! First it's Tony Blair blatherin' on about a 'Yes' vote, then John Major, then Hague. Who is it now?"

Tony Blair appeared alongside his former political foe John Major to kick-start the campaign for a 'yes' vote in the Northern Ireland referendum on the Good Friday Agreement.

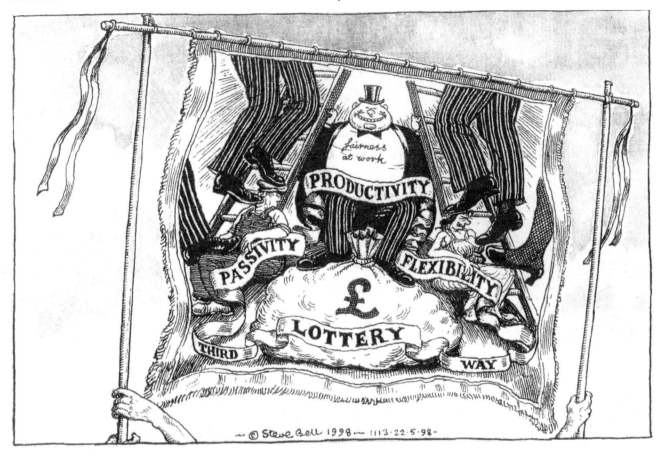

The long awaited Fairness at Work White Paper was announced in the Commons by Margaret Beckett.
The proposals went further than most union leaders and employers expected and guaranteed a new
set of workplace and union rights for employees.

'It's your wife, Mr Paisley, sir. Are you coming home soon? This is your sixth recount.'

The referendum on the Good Friday Agreement in Northern Ireland resulted in a resounding 'yes' with the support of over 70% of the voters.

Hague's reshuffle of the Shadow Cabinet provided some surprising returns to the front bench. Ann Widdecombe was appointed to Health, apparently with the brief of bringing the Tories back in touch with ordinary people. Other appointments proved less surprising, Norman Fowler as Shadow Home Secretary, Cecil Parkinson as Chairman of the Conservative Party, Peter Lilley as Deputy Leader, John Redwood as Shadow Trade and Industry, Gillian Shephard as Shadow Environment, Transport and the Regions and Francis Maude as Shadow Chancellor. Paul Gascoigne was earlier dropped from the England World Cup football team for being unfit. He had been criticised in the press, frequently, for being overweight and drinking too much.

The Chancellor, Gordon Brown, prompted anger amongst the unions and the Labour left,
when he signalled that he intended to keep the straitjacket on public spending in place until the
next General Election. Many backbenchers expected to see the two-year restraints on public
spending relaxed in July.

More rebellion on Labour's back-benches against the government's plans to charge university students
£1,000 a year in tuition fees.

Andrew Mackinlay, the Labour MP for Thurrock, delighted many in the Commons with a question at Prime Minister's Question Time, in which he urged Tony Blair to discourage sycophantic and fawning questions from his benches, and to encourage scrutiny and accountability.

The Bank of England was criticised by the unions, business, the City and the Opposition, after its
surprise decision to push up interest rates was condemned as risking turning an economic slowdown
into full-scale recession.

Diplomats began planning an emergency meeting, and NATO considered military action to seal the
border between Kosovo and Albania, amidst reports of 50 dead, 200 missing and mass graves in
Kosovo. Tony Blair warned Slobodan Milosevic, the nationalist Serb leader, that the European Union
considered the situation to be very serious.

It was reported that dustcarts that weigh and keep a record of each household's rubbish may soon appear on British streets as part of a new charging scheme to increase recycling. In the run-up to candidate selection for the post of Mayor of London, the two main hopefuls, Jeffrey Archer and Ken Livingstone were becoming less confident. Conservative chiefs decided to subject Lord Archer of Weston-super-Mare to the first investigation by its ethics and integrity committee should he stand. Ken Livingstone, former leader of the GLC, was ruled out by the Labour leadership for fear he would embark on a left wing agenda.

TRY THIS:— BLAIR'S BLUES CORNER NO.1

• WOKE UP THIS MORNIN'
WITH them MINIMUM WAGE'S BLUES
BLEW ALL MA CHANCES
AIN'T GOT NOTHIN' TO LOSE

12 MONTHS IN POWER
and THEY'RE BEATING' ON
ME —
GONNA START TAXIN'
PEOPLE'S GENEROSITY

He also
SERVES etc

Gordon Brown announced in the Commons the sale of twelve billion pounds of state assets to a silent Labour backbench.

England's opening World Cup match in Marseilles was marred by riots by English football fans, and violent clashes with riot police and Tunisian supporters.

'It's no use moaning to me, Doris. You should let the Prime Minister
know how you feel about the minimum wage.'

The Government's decision to set a national minimum wage at £3.60 per hour excluded part-time
workers, apprentices and the under-eighteens will have no guaranteed minimum at all. Bill Morris
of the Transport and General Workers Union described the decision as "an endorsement of
workplace poverty".

William Hague reached his first anniversary as Leader of the Conservative Party amidst a week of
fevered speculation about plots to unseat him.

David Blunkett, Secretary of State for Education, announced the first twenty-five Education Action
Zones in the radical overhaul of England's schools. Education Action Zones will allow any
organisation, private or public, to bid to run groups of schools.

Alastair Campbell, the Prime Minister's Chief Press Secretary, appeared before the government's
Public Administration Committee and denied describing the Chancellor to journalists as
"psychologically flawed".

"The onward march of democracy."

The elections for the Ulster Assembly presented the first opportunity to the people of Northern Ireland since 1972 to shape a devolved administration.

Tony Blair's relationship with *The Sun* soured as the paper printed a front page picture of the Prime
Minister next to the banner headline: "Is this the most dangerous man in Britain?" The attack was
triggered by Blair's apparent sympathy for a European single currency.

A report by Saferworld, an independent research group, stated that the government had approved
more than 2,000 licences for arms exports to some of the world's most volatile trouble spots in
apparent breach of its ethical foreign policy guidelines.

St Tony downloading from Cyberspace to heal the sick & bring succour to the people of Ulster

Tony Blair marked the fiftieth anniversary of the NHS by launching the NHS Modernisation Fund. He outlined a vision of the future in which doctors could be consulted on the Internet and heart monitoring could be done over the phone. Blair later flew to Belfast in an attempt to defuse the growing crisis about the Orange Order's planned march through Drumcree.

The Parades Commission announced that it was going to ban the Orangemen's traditional parade,
which would take them through the Nationalist area of the Garvaghy Road in Drumcree.

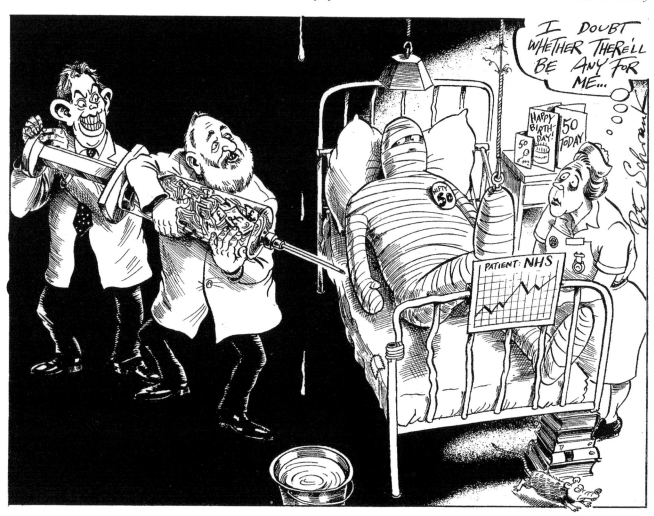

On the fiftieth anniversary of its establishment, Tony Blair announced an extra eight billion pounds for
the National Health Service. The money, however, will be directed into cutting waiting lists and
improving services rather than meeting demands for public sector pay rises.

England crashed out of the World Cup after losing on penalties to Argentina after a 2 – 2 draw. The
problems dogging Blair's premiership rumbled on.

Tony Blair slipped comfortably on to the Des O'Connor Show's sofa, dropped a vowel or two, and
reinforced his media image as a man of the people.

Derek Draper, lobbyist and former Labour party aide, accused of selling access to ministers, admitted he had been brash and boastful about his contacts with ministers and government advisers. Tony Blair, in an effort to deflect accusations of sleaze, urged his ministers and advisers to be "purer than pure".

The government's reform of the House of Lords which proposed to end the six-hundred-year-old right
of hereditary peers to sit and vote in the Upper House was criticised by members of the Opposition
for not proposing an adequate replacement.

Senior Orangemen met Tony Blair at Downing Street in an effort to defuse the crisis at Drumcree.
Blair made it clear, however, that he would not overturn the ruling made by the Parades Commission.

The Observer, which broke the 'cash for access' story, stated that "faxes went almost every day" from the office of Peter Mandelson to his former aide Derek Draper at the lobbying firm GPC Market Access.

BIGOT'S CUP '98

The eight-day protest at Drumcree, held by members of the Orange Order culminated in a loyalist arson attack on a Catholic home which killed three children.

1. Buying Britain

2. Listening to Britain

"The Ratings Game."

The Chancellor Gordon Brown announced a three-year public spending plan of fifty-six billion pounds to be spent on health and education. The announcement was the centrepiece of the Comprehensive Spending Review, a year-long study which involved over one thousand meetings. William Hague also launched the Conservative Party's 'Listening to Britain' campaign which took him round the country to hear the views of the people.